PETS TO THE RESCUE

Ringo Saves the Day!

A True Story

SIMON SPOTLIGHT
An imprint of Simon & Schuster Children's Publishing Division
1230 Avenue of the Americas, New York, New York 10020
First Simon Spotlight paperback edition July 2011
Text copyright © 2001 by Andrew Clements
Illustrations copyright © 2001 by Ellen Beier

SIMON SPOTLIGHT, READY-TO-READ, and colophon are
registered trademarks of Simon & Schuster, Inc.
For information about special discounts for bulk purchases, please
contact Simon & Schuster Special Sales at 1-866-506-1949 or
business@simonandschuster.com.
The text of this book was set in Times New Roman.
The illustrations were rendered in watercolor.
Manufactured in the United States of America 1119 LAK
20 19 18 17 16 15
Library of Congress Cataloging-in-Publication Data
Clements, Andrew, 1949–
Ringo saves the day! / written by Andrew Clements ;
illustrated by Ellen Beier
p. cm.–(Pets to the Rescue)
Summary: A young woman and her husband are glad that they gave a
stray kitten a home when it saves their lives by alerting them to a gas leak.
1. Cats–Anecdotes–Juvenile literature. [1. Cats. 2. Pets.] I. Beier, Ellen, ill.
II. Title. III. Series.
SF445.7.C59 2000   636.8/0887 21   99-039044
ISBN 978-0-689-83439-4 (pbk)
ISBN 978-1-4814-1495-1 (eBook)

PETS TO THE RESCUE

Ringo Saves the Day!

A True Story

Written by Andrew Clements
Illustrated by Ellen Beier

Ready-to-Read

Simon Spotlight
New York   London   Toronto   Sydney   New Delhi

Carol went to visit her mother
at a nursing home.
She saw a cat in the woods.

The cat did not have a home.
And it did not have much
of a tail.

Paul lived at the nursing home.
He gave the cat bits of food.
He told Carol, "We call the cat
Mitzi."

Mitzi was getting bigger.
She was going to have kittens.

Carol brought food for Mitzi.
The food helped the kittens
inside her grow.

One day, no one saw Mitzi.

She was not in the yard.

She was not by the woods.

Then Paul found her.
Mitzi had four new kittens!

Carol wanted the small
orange kitten.
It reminded her of a plump
little pumpkin.

But Carol and her husband Ray
had three other cats.

She said, "We do not need
another one."

But a big dog lived
at the nursing home.
This dog did not like cats.
Mitzi and her kittens had to go
live somewhere else.

14

Carol said, "We will take
the orange kitten home."

And they did.

The new kitten was smart.
When he wanted to go out,
he went tap-tap-tap-tap.

He was like a drummer.
Carol named him Ringo.

Ringo grew

and grew

and grew.

Then Carol and Ray
got very sick.

They felt sleepy all the time.

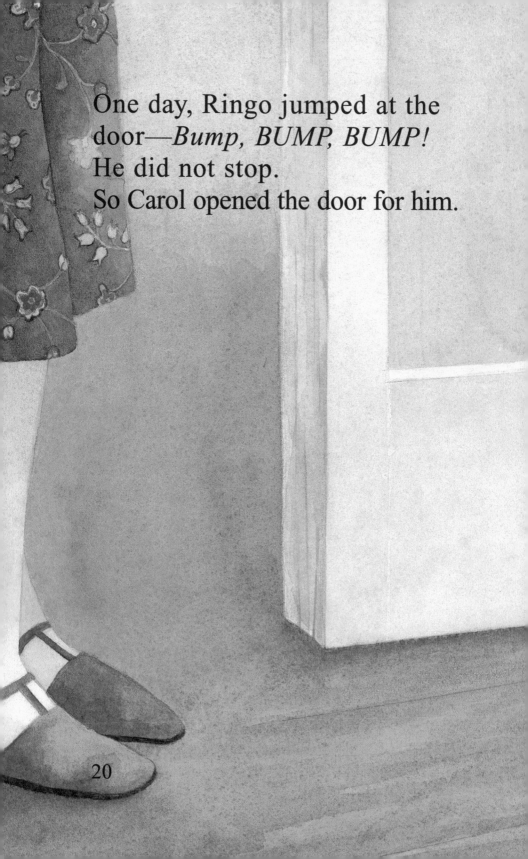

One day, Ringo jumped at the
door—*Bump, BUMP, BUMP!*
He did not stop.
So Carol opened the door for him.

Ringo went out.
"Meow! Meow!"
Ringo wanted Carol to come out.
When Carol went out,
Ringo started to walk.

Then he stopped.
"Meow! Meow!"
Ringo wanted Carol
to follow him.

Ringo led Carol
around the house.
He started to dig in some rocks.
Ringo had never
done that before.

Ringo stopped digging.
"Meow! Meow!"
Ringo wanted Carol to come.

Carol went onto the rocks.
Then she knew why Ringo
was digging.
Carol smelled gas.

It was the kind of gas
that can blow up!
Carol went into the house.
She called for help.
Some men came fast.

The men started to dig
right where Ringo did.
They found a broken gas pipe.

One man said, "It's a good thing you found this!"

Carol said, "I did not find it. Ringo found it!"

The gas had made
Carol and Ray very sick.
It almost made their house
blow up.
Ringo had saved them.

Carol and Ray told people
about Ringo.
Ringo was a hero.
He was even on TV.

A rich man heard about Ringo.
He called Carol.
He said, "Will you sell Ringo
to me?
I will pay you a lot of money."

Carol told the man, "We would never sell Ringo.
Ringo is part of our family!"